CAPTAIN FACT's

DINOSAUR ADVENTURE

BY
KNIFE & PACKER

EGMONT

KNIFE & PACKER FACT!

IF KNIFE AND PACKER COULD INVITE ANY DINOSAUR
ROUND FOR DINNER IT WOULD HAVE TO BE THE
DIPLODOCUS. HIS INCREDIBLY LONG NECK AND
TAIL WOULD MAKE HIM GREAT FUN TO
DRAW - AND HE WOULD EAT ALL
THE GREENS!

First published in Great Britain in 2004
by Egmont Books Limited, 239 Kensington High Street, London W8 6SA

Text and illustrations copyright © 2004 Knife and Packer
The moral rights of the authors have been asserted.

ISBN 1 4052 0833 3

1 3 5 7 9 10 8 6 4 2

A CIP catalogue record for this title is available
from the British Library

Printed and bound in Great Britain

CONTENTS

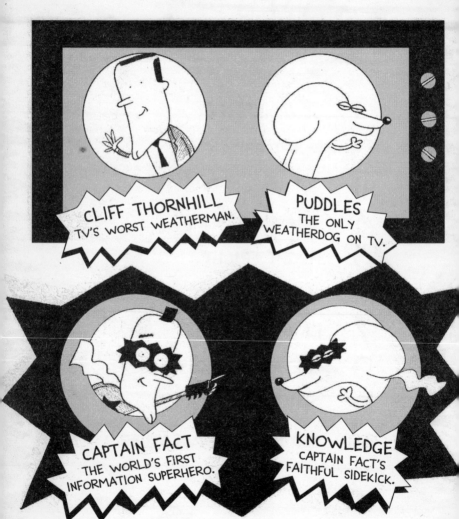

RiNG...

LUCY
HEAD OF MAKE-UP AND
CLIFF'S BEST FRIEND.

THE BOSS
HE'S SCARY!

PROFESSOR MINISCULE
HEAD OF THE FACT CAVE
AND THE BRAINS BEHIND MISSIONS.

FACTORELLA
PROFESSOR MINISCULE'S
DAUGHTER AND ALL-ROUND
WHIZZ-KID.

CHAPTER 1
DINO-DISASTER

TV'S WORST WEATHERMAN, Cliff Thornhill, and his sidekick, Puddles the dog, were in their office playing their favourite computer game, 'Dinosaur Attack III'.

'This is great,' said Cliff. 'I love it when the Boss is on holiday!'

'Game over!' said Knowledge. 'I keep being eaten by the Tyrannosaurus Rex – those dinosaurs are terrifying!'

'It's not the dinosaurs, it's you,' said Cliff. 'Let me have a go.'

Just as Cliff picked up the controls there was a loud knock at the door.

Before Cliff could even say 'come in', the door burst open. There stood the Boss – and he wasn't in a happy holiday mood . . .

'Thornhill, you're useless!' he shouted. 'You predicted two weeks of boiling hot sunshine.'

'Don't tell me it rained?' asked Cliff sheepishly.

'Rain?! It rained so much I had to use a snorkel just to get to my bedroom! In fact it was so awful that I decided to come back early.'

'It's great to have you back,' mumbled Cliff as the Boss slammed the door.

'Phew!' said Puddles, who only spoke when there was no one else around. 'Lucky he didn't spot the video game.'

Just then there was another knock at the door. 'HIDE!' shouted Cliff. He and Puddles ducked under the desk.

'Cliff? Puddles? What are you doing down there?' Luckily it wasn't the Boss, it was Lucy, Cliff's friend from the Make-up Department.

Cliff and Puddles gingerly emerged from under the desk.

'Have you seen the news? A dinosaur egg has hatched at the museum!' said Lucy.

'That's amazing – a real live dinosaur!' said Cliff, blushing. Cliff often blushed when Lucy was around. 'Aren't they supposed to be extinct?'

'Yes, and this little dinosaur soon will be too, without her mother,' said Lucy sadly.

'Right,' said Puddles, as soon as Lucy had left the office, 'back to Dinosaur Attack III – this time I'm going to beat those scary dinosaurs.'

'Never mind that, Puddles,' said Cliff. 'It's time you met a *real* dinosaur! Because THIS IS A . . .'

'Not so fast!' interrupted Puddles. 'I'm going to say it . . .'

'Well get a move on!' said Cliff.

Puddles coughed theatrically. 'THIS IS A MISSION FOR CAPTAIN FACT!' And with that he jumped off his chair and yanked on the lever to reveal the pole to the Fact Cave . . .

FACT CAVE

CAPTAIN FACT

KNOWLEDGE

'We've got to save that dinosaur!' said Captain Fact as they ran down the corridors to the Fact Cave Nerve Centre…

'I'm not sure if I want to meet a real live dinosaur,' said Knowledge.

'Don't worry, I'm sure she'll like you,' said Captain Fact.

'What – barbequed or broiled?' asked Knowledge nervously.

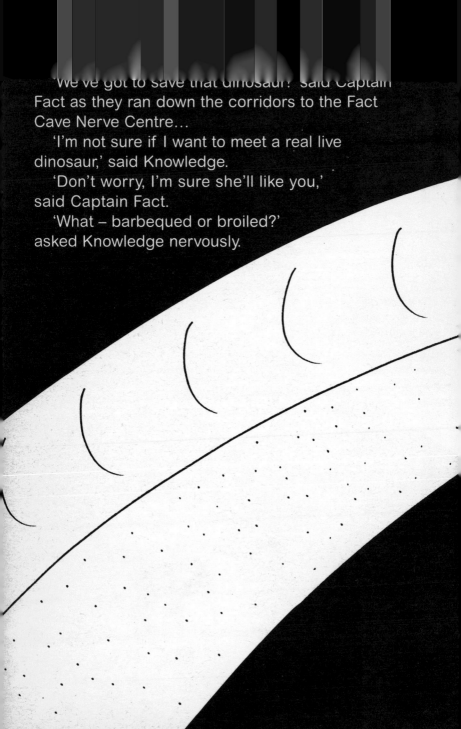

'Why can't the museum just take the baby dinosaur to the zoo?' asked Knowledge. 'Surely they'd be able to look after her. They look after lizards and crocodiles all the time, don't they?'

'What you need are some baby dinosaur facts,' said Captain Fact, as his nose began to tremble . . .

'So you see, Knowledge, we're going to have to reunite the baby dinosaur with her mother,' said Captain Fact as he opened the door of the Nerve Centre.

'That's all very well,' said Knowledge, 'but how are we going to go back millions of years to the time of the dinosaurs?'

CHAPTER 2
BLAST BACK

'CAPTAIN FACT AND Knowledge, there you are!' said Professor Miniscule, emerging from behind a large box. Professor Miniscule, the world's shortest genius and the Fact Cave's planner-in-chief, wasn't one for small talk.

'Aaaaagh!' screamed Knowledge, leaping into Captain Fact's arms, 'there's a huge green cat in there!'

'That's no cat,' said Professor Miniscule. 'Meet Tricky the baby Triceratops – Tricky, this is Captain Fact and Knowledge. They're going to reunite you with your mother.'

'Eeek,' said Tricky, who spoke in baby dinosaur squeaks.

'Does she bite?' asked Knowledge nervously.

'Don't be ridiculous Knowledge,' said Captain Fact. 'Ker-Fact! Triceratops are herbivorous. That means they only eat plant matter. You know, cabbage, broccoli, brussels sprouts . . .'

'Yuuuuck, that's disgusting,' said Knowledge.

'Enough!' interrupted Miniscule. 'There's no time to waste. The Museum has entrusted me with Tricky – you're her only hope.'

'I've invented the world's first fully functioning time machine. It will take you and Tricky back to the time of the dinosaurs!' said Miniscule proudly.

'Amazing!' said Captain Fact. 'You've actually built a time machine that works?'

'Most of the time . . .' mumbled Professor Miniscule.

'Most of the time? What do you mean, most of the time?' asked Captain Fact anxiously.

Just then, much to Professor Miniscule's relief, Factorella bounced in.

'When are we off, Dad?' asked Factorella excitedly. 'I've been reading all about dinosaurs and I can't wait to go!'

'You know you're too young to go on missions, Factorella,' sighed Professor Miniscule. 'You've still got years of training ahead of you before you can become a superhero. Now, what have you come up with on dinosaurs?'

Factorella looked glum, but turned to Factotum, the Fact Cave's Super Computer.

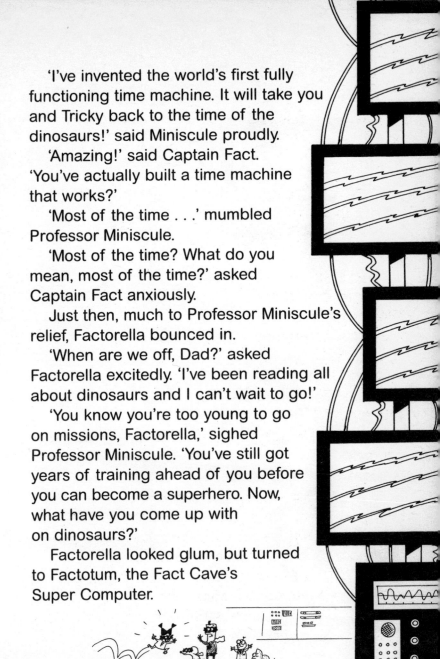

JURASSIC PERIOD: WET AND WARM WITH HUGE FLOODS. LOTS OF PLANTS MEANT THAT MASSIVE PLANT-EATING DINOSAURS EVOLVED. THE FIRST BIRDS APPEARED. *208-144 MILLION YEARS AGO*

CRETACEOUS PERIOD: EXPLOSIVE GROWTH IN LIFE AND LOTS OF DINOSAURS. THE FIRST SNAKES, MODERN MAMMALS AND FLOWERING PLANTS APPEARED. *144-65 MILLION YEARS AGO*

'What's the matter, Knowledge? You're looking a bit pale,' said Captain Fact.

'I get the feeling we're going to bump into quite a few of these dinosaurs,' snivelled Knowledge.

'When you've quite finished,' said Miniscule, 'I'd like to show you something special . . .' And with that he pressed a large red button and the floor and walls began to shudder . . .

'This is my finest creation: THE PAST BLASTER 3000.'

In front of them stood a gleaming time machine.

'Take your seats and prepare for the journey of a lifetime,' said Miniscule.

Captain Fact, Knowledge and Tricky approached the machine as Factorella looked on enviously.

'You said it worked most of the time?' asked Captain Fact, 'What did you mean by that?'

'Well, it does have a habit of occasionally missing the intended time period,' replied Miniscule as he shoved them in the direction of the time machine. 'Now please take your seats.'

'Occasionally missing the intended time period!' said Captain Fact anxiously. 'That means we could end up anywhere!'

But with the engines fired up it was too noisy for Professor Miniscule to hear him . . .

SECRET FACT!

HOW DID CAPTAIN FACT MEET KNOWLEDGE?

CLIFF THORNHILL LOVED THE CIRCUS . . .

CIRCUS

IT WAS THE BIGGEST TREAT OF THE YEAR AND CLIFF NEVER MISSED IT . . .

TICKETS

ONE YEAR, ON HIS SEVENTH BIRTHDAY, THERE WAS A NEW ACT IN THE SHOW . . .

AND NOW - WOOFO THE WONDER DOG, THE CLUED-UP CANINE!

BUT CLIFF COULD SEE THAT WOOFO WAS UNHAPPY . . .

COME ON! THE CAPITAL OF EQUADOR IS???

IN FACT HE SEEMED SO UNHAPPY THAT CLIFF DECIDED TO DOGNAP HIM . . .

HE RENAMED HIM PUDDLES AND THEY'VE BEEN BEST FRIENDS EVER SINCE . . .

(ALTHOUGH AT THE TIME THEY HAD NO IDEA THEY'D GO ON TO BECOME THE WORLD'S GREATEST SUPERHEROES AS CAPTAIN FACT AND KNOWLEDGE.)

CHAPTER 3
UG!

AS THE PAST Blaster 3000 flew back in time, our three intrepid time travellers were shaken, shuddered and thoroughly wobbled.

Suddenly the time machine juddered to a halt.

'Wow, that was some journey!' gasped Captain Fact, adjusting his mask.

'It was like being in a giant washing machine,' panted Knowledge. 'I feel like a pair of soggy socks.'

'Professor Miniscule warned us that this machine makes mistakes,' said Captain Fact as he looked around but before he could work out where they were, Tricky started making strange squeaks.

'Maybe she's trying to tell us something?' said Knowledge. Suddenly there was a loud cracking noise . . .

'A dinosaur's trying to climb aboard!'
screamed Knowledge.

'That's not a dinosaur,
it's a woolly mammoth!'
said Captain Fact worriedly.
'RUN!' Captain Fact swept
up Tricky and they all jumped
out of the time machine and
made a dash for it.

'Let's hide in this cave,' suggested Knowledge.

'Ker-Fact! We haven't gone back far enough,'
said Captain Fact, slightly out of breath. 'Woolly
mammoths lived in the Quaternary period.' And
with that his elbow began to itch . . .

'Let's wait here until the mammoths have moved on,' said Captain Fact peering out of the entrance to the cave.

'I'm starving,' said Knowledge. 'Where do you get dog biscuits around here? I know – I'll ask that man over there.'

'MAN?' Captain Fact spun round. Right behind them stood a caveman.

'Ug!' said the caveman, who had never met a superhero before.

'Ug!' said Captain Fact, who had never met a caveman before.

Fortunately the caveman seemed friendly and held out an enormous chunk of charred woolly-rhino meat.

'Disgusting!' said Knowledge grimacing.

'Er . . . thank you. That's very kind,' said Captain Fact, not wishing to offend the caveman. 'I'll put it in my bag for later . . .'

'You don't have any woolly-rhino-flavoured dog biscuits, do you?' asked Knowledge.

'Don't be ridiculous, Knowledge,' said Captain Fact, as his nose began to twitch . . .

Much as they were enjoying the company of their new prehistoric friend, Captain Fact and Knowledge were on a mission.

'Looks like those mammoths have gone,' said Captain Fact. 'Let's go back to the time machine.'

Keeping a wary look out they returned to the Past Blaster 3000.

'Goodbye, Caveman,' said Captain Fact.

'Ug-bye,' said the caveman as he brushed away a tear.

Once again the three time travellers took their seats . . .

UG-BYE!

CHAPTER 4
TRIASSIC TERROR

AS THE TIME machine whirred and spun, a familiar voice came through on the intercom.

'Professor Miniscule here – *crackle* – sorry about that detour – *pop* – but I should warn you I'm still having some technical problems with the time machine – *fizz* . . .'

Before Captain Fact could protest, the Past Blaster 3000 ground to a screeching halt.

'Let's hope this is the right time target,' said Captain Fact unconvinced.

They looked out over a glittering lagoon surrounded by palm trees.

'I don't care what time target this is, check out the beach!' said Knowledge excitedly. 'Let's swim!'

As Knowledge jumped into the inviting water Tricky started making the strange squeaking noise again.

'I wouldn't do that if I were you,' said Captain Fact as Knowledge frolicked happily in the warm water.

'What do you mean? It's lovely in here!' said Knowledge.

'I think when Tricky squeaks it's a warning,' said Captain Fact. 'WATCH OUT KNOWLEDGE – BEHIND YOU!'

'I've never seen you move so fast,' said Captain Fact as Knowledge overtook him.

'What was that?' asked Knowledge.

'I have a horrible feeling that was Nothosaurus,' said Captain Fact, 'I think we might be in the Triassic period!'

'Still,' said Knowledge, looking on the bright side, 'at least we're safe in these palm trees.' Just then there was a rustle in the bushes . . .

'That's definitely Lagosuchus,' said Captain Fact as a motley crew of skinny, long-legged reptiles made a dash for them. 'They might be only 40 centimetres long but I don't like the look of them.'

'Quick, throw them that woolly-rhino meat that the caveman gave us,' said Knowledge.

'Ker-Fact! We've gone back 60 million years too far!' said Captain Fact as he tossed the mass of ravenous reptiles the meaty bone. 'Whilst they're having lunch let's make a dash to the Past Blaster 3000.'

'It's even scarier than I thought!' wheezed Knowledge as they beat a hasty retreat from the Triassic period. 'How on earth did other dinosaurs survive with predators like these around?'

'Dinosaurs had all kinds of self-defence tricks up their sleeves,' said Captain Fact as his earlobes began to wobble . . .

FACT

DINO TRUMPS NEW

NAME:
ANKYLOSAURUS

SPECIAL WEAPON:
ARMOUR-PLATED SKIN AND SPIKEY BACK

POWER:
AN UNPLEASANT MOUTHFUL FOR ANY PREDATOR

TERROR RATING:
***** CRUNCHY ON THE OUTSIDE!

NAME:
IGUANODON

SPECIAL WEAPON:
SPIKED THUMB

POWER:
GOUGING – IDEAL FOR SELF DEFENCE

TERROR RATING:
***** THUMBS UP TO IGUANODON!

NAME:
DEINONYCHUS

SPECIAL WEAPON:
GIANT CLAW ON SECOND TOE

POWER:
GOOD FOR HUNTING AND
FISHING AS WELL AS
SLASHING AND
RIPPING!

TERROR RATING:
*** DUCK!

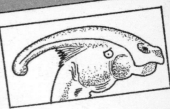

NAME:
PARASAUROLOPHUS

SPECIAL WEAPON:
HOLLOW SKULL CREST COULD
MAKE LOUD NOISE

POWER:
COULD ALERT HERD AND SCARE
OFF PREDATORS

HONK!

TERROR RATING:
*** EAR PLUGS IN!

NAME:
STEGOSAURUS

SPECIAL WEAPON:
TAIL CLUB

POWER:
TAIL COULD BE USED LIKE A
WHIP – SOME EVEN HAD
SPIKES!

TERROR RATING:
*** OUCH!

ATTACK!!!

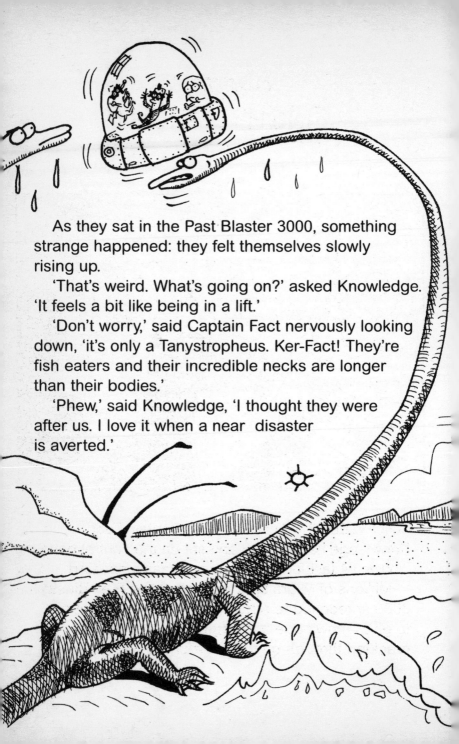

As they sat in the Past Blaster 3000, something strange happened: they felt themselves slowly rising up.

'That's weird. What's going on?' asked Knowledge. 'It feels a bit like being in a lift.'

'Don't worry,' said Captain Fact nervously looking down, 'it's only a Tanystropheus. Ker-Fact! They're fish eaters and their incredible necks are longer than their bodies.'

'Phew,' said Knowledge, 'I thought they were after us. I love it when a near disaster is averted.'

CHAPTER 5
FLIGHT FRIGHT

'KNOWLEDGE, NO!' SHOUTED Captain Fact.
Knowledge had slipped and sat on the control panel.
'You've hit fast forwaaaaaaaaaaaaaaaaaaaaaaaard . . .'

Millions of years spun by before the Past Blaster
3000 screeched to a halt. Captain Fact was about
to give Knowledge a telling-off when a voice
crackled through on the intercom . . .

'Professor Miniscule here – *pop* – thanks to Knowledge's bottom you're in the Jurassic period - *crackle* – you're 100 million years off target – *fizz* – I'm going to re-calibrate the navigation – *whirr* – whatever you do – *crackle* - do not leave the time machine.'

'That's a shame,' said Knowledge. 'It looks nice and warm out there. Look at all those trees and plants.'

'Right – *crackle* - brace yourselves and prepare to blast off . . .'

'STOP!' shouted Captain Fact. 'Where's Tricky?' Tricky was nowhere to be seen.

'Professor Miniscule, Tricky seems to have made a dash for it,' said Captain Fact. 'It looks as though we'll have to take a closer look at the Jurassic. We'll be back as soon as we can.'

And with that they jumped out of the Past Blaster 3000 and started searching for Tricky.

Captain Fact and Knowledge searched and searched in the dense Jurassic undergrowth. They were just about to give up when they heard a familiar squeak.

'It's Tricky!' said Captain Fact spotting their missing Triceratops.

'Why is it getting dark all of a sudden?' asked Knowledge. 'That's the biggest cloud I've ever seen.'

'I don't think that's a cloud, Knowledge,' said Captain Fact, as his knees began to knock . . .

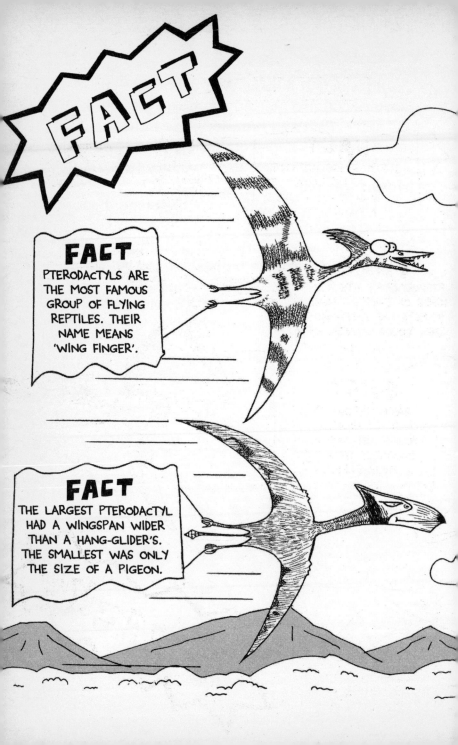

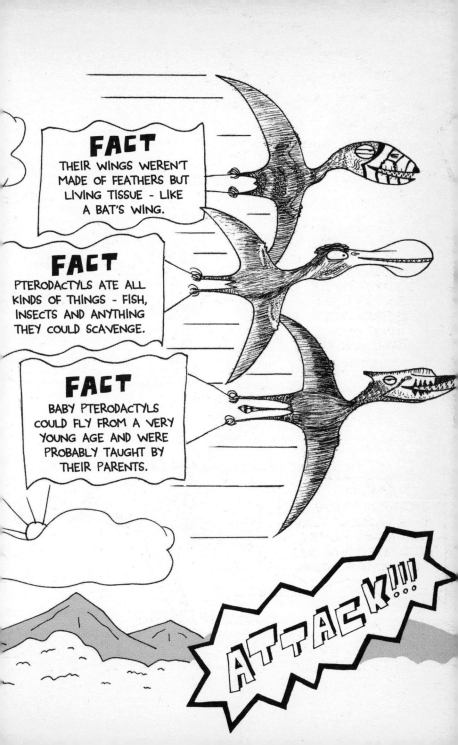

Captain Fact had barely finished his Fact Attack
when they were all swept off the ground by a flock
of angry Pterodactyls.

'Hang on tight, we're coming in to land!' warned
Captain Fact.

'Phew,' said Knowledge. 'That's a relief. And look,
lovely little baby Pterodactyls. They're so cute!'

'Cute but hungry,' said Captain Fact. 'And I think
we're on the menu!'

And with that the Pterodactyls dropped
Captain Fact, Knowledge and Tricky amongst the
peckish chicks.

'Hello, friendly Pterodactyls,' said Knowledge nervously. 'You don't want to eat us, do you? Look, I'm horrible and furry and he's wearing tights – yuk.'

'Ker-Fact! Pterodactyl young are fed on regurgitated and partly digested food,' said Captain Fact gratefully.

'That's sick,' said Knowledge.

'Literally,' said Captain Fact. 'So before their parents decide to gobble us up and regurgitate us, let's get out of here. I've got a plan . . .'

'You're going to have to trust me on this one, Knowledge,' said Captain Fact grabbing a large discarded fish tail.

'You know I hate heights,' said Knowledge as Tricky looked gingerly over the edge of the cliff.

'Sorry, Knowledge, but it's heights or regurgitation,' said Captain Fact. They all grabbed hold of the tail and jumped . . .

CHAPTER 6
JURASSIC JAWS

'MUCH AS I like your improvised glider idea,' said Knowledge, 'there is one little thing. Where are we going to land?'

'Erm . . . I hadn't thought of that,' replied Captain Fact realizing they were miles from shore and heading straight out to sea.

'After meeting that Nothosaurus in the Triassic I've gone off the idea of prehistoric swimming,' said Knowledge anxiously.

'Wait a minute, what's that down there?' said Captain Fact. 'It's an island – we're saved!!!'

Captain Fact, Knowledge and Tricky glided down on to the surface of a small, round island.

'Strange,' said Captain Fact, 'it just seemed to appear . . .'

'. . . And it feels like it's moving,' said Knowledge smelling something fishy.

'Yes, we do appear to be floating along,' said Captain Fact looking nervously at the churning water. 'And I wonder if all prehistoric islands have four legs and a heaaaaaaaaaaad!'

'I do believe we're on the back of some sort of turtle,' said Captain Fact. 'Ker-Fact! Prehistoric turtles such as Archelon could reach a size of four metres long and weigh up to three tonnes!'

'Still, at least we're heading in the right direction,' said Knowledge. 'What could possibly go wrong now?'

Just then Tricky cleared her throat . . .

'Oh dear,' said Captain Fact, 'I've got a bad feeling about this . . .'

A huge, gaping mouth loomed out of the sea.

'What's that?' screamed Knowledge.

'Ker-Fact! It's Liopleurodon, one of the most terrifying marine predators of all time, and I get the distinct impression that his favourite snack may be Turtle Surprise,' replied Captain Fact.

'I think it's safe to say we're in a sticky pickle,' said Knowledge.

'Pickles don't get much stickier,' said Captain Fact. 'Looks like we're going to have to call Professor Miniscule!' And with that he pressed the emergency button on his Fact Watch.

Just as the jaws were about to close on the turtle sandwich, Factorella appeared in a flash.

'You were lucky Dad had already sent me back to the Jurrassic era,' said Factorella. 'I've been repairing the Past Blaster 3000. Isn't it great here? Dinosaurs everywhere! By the way, how did it get that dent on the control panel? Looks like one of you sat on it.'

'Erm, really?' winced Knowledge.

'Well, it's repaired now,' said Factorella, 'I'll hold out here until you're on dry land, then I've got to blast back to the Fact Cave – Dad's baking a cake and I'll be in trouble if I'm not back in time for tea. Good luck with the mission!'

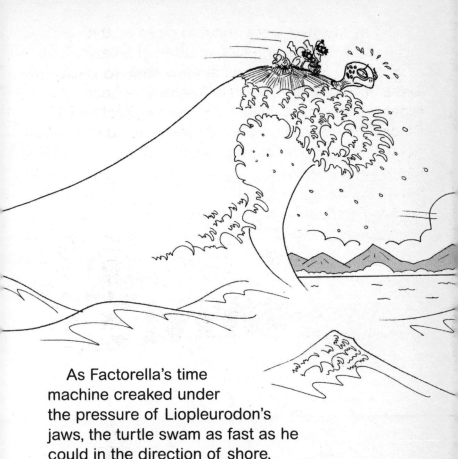

As Factorella's time
machine creaked under
the pressure of Liopleurodon's
jaws, the turtle swam as fast as he
could in the direction of shore.

'To think I used to be scared of sharks,' said
Knowledge. 'I wonder what else is lurking out there?'

'Funny you should ask that,' replied Captain
Fact, as his ears began to twitch . . .

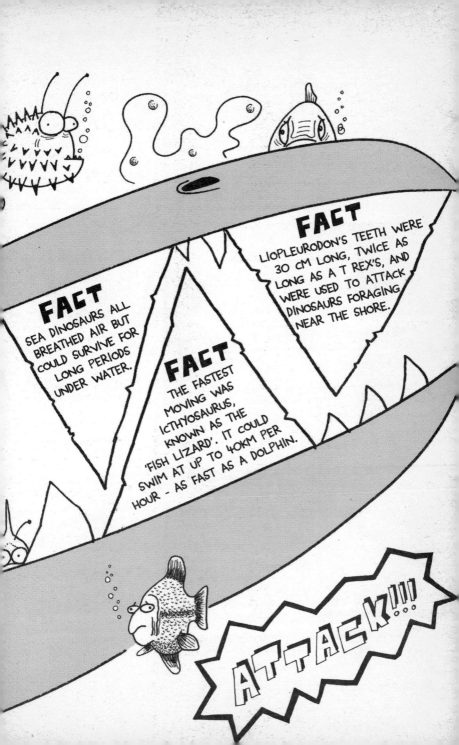

At last they reached shore. In the distance they saw a flash of light.

'That'll be Factorella heading back to the Fact Cave,' said Captain Fact as he waved fondly in the direction of the Liopleurodon.

BANG!

CHAPTER 7
LAVA PALAVER

'LOOK AT THE Past Blaster 3000!' said Knowledge
as they approached their polished and shiny time
machine.

'Now that Factorella's fixed it we should have no
problem getting to the Cretaceous period,' said
Captain Fact as he started the machine up. 'You'll
be with your mum in no time, Tricky.'

'Look – Factorella even left me some dog biscuits.
Curry-flavoured, my favourite!' said Knowledge.

With a flourish Captain Fact pressed the take-off
button. Once again they were travelling through time.

As they juddered to a halt the intercom sprang to life.

'*Fizz* – Welcome to the Cretaceous Period gentlemen – *crackle* – at last!' said Professor Miniscule. 'Now all you've got to – *fizz* – do is find Tricky's mother.'

'Wow! It's lovely out here,' said Knowledge as he scanned the lush landscape that surrounded them.

'There's no time to admire the view, Knowledge,' said Captain Fact. 'Now we're in the right time period we've got to get Tricky home.'

68

Just then the ground began to shake.
'Is that your stomach rumbling?'
asked Knowledge.
'No! It's a VOLCANO!' shouted
Captain Fact.

RUN!

All around them dinosaurs
were fleeing the advancing lava.

'We're going to be swept away!' panted
Knowledge.

'There's only one thing for it,' said Captain Fact.
'Let's get on the back of this Diplodocus.'

'How are we going to get up there? It's HUGE!'
screeched Knowledge.

'Ker-Fact! Diplodocus are over five metres tall!
The tail, use the tail . . .' urged Captain Fact.

Grabbing Tricky, Captain Fact and
Knowledge ran up the tail of the Diplodocus.

'Now hang on a minute,' said Knowledge. 'We've
spent most of this mission running away from
dinosaurs, and now you've got us running up
them!'

'Oh, there's nothing to worry about,' said Captain
Fact as his toes began to tremble . . .

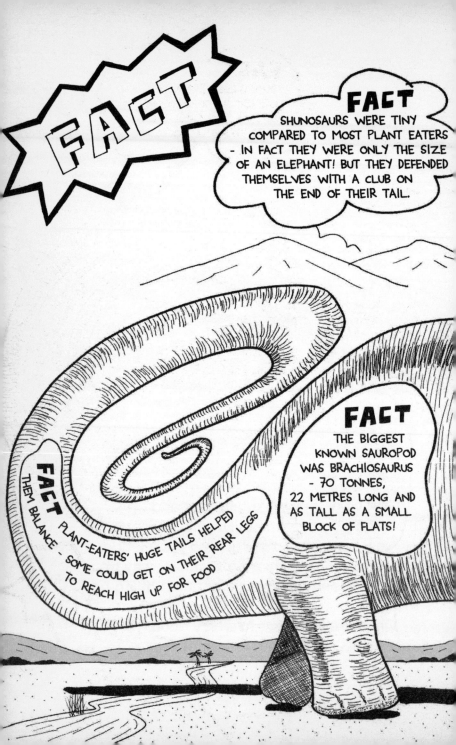

'Amazing!' said Knowledge. 'But none of those creatures is Tricky's mother.'

'That's right, Knowledge,' said Captain Fact, 'and now we need to find her.'

CHAPTER 8
CRETACEOUS CRITTERS

WHEN THEY WERE a safe distance away from the volcano they slid off the back of the Diplodocus.

'Aren't the Triceratops in the phone book?' asked Knowledge

'Knowledge, really! We're going to have to use the Power of Fact,' said Captain Fact. 'Ker-Fact! Triceratops moved around in huge herds.'

'So we're looking for a large group of enormous dinosaurs,' said Knowledge. In the distance there was a strange knocking noise. 'And they'll be playing baseball?'

'Er, no,' said Captain Fact, 'but I think we should investigate.'

In a clearing were the strangest looking dinosaurs they'd seen yet.

'What on earth are those?' asked Knowledge, 'they look like mad professors.'

'Ker-Fact! That's Pachycephalosaurus, the biggest of the "bone heads", ' said Captain Fact. 'That knocking noise was them battering their heads together – it's their way of fighting and frightening off enemies.'

'Ouch!' said Knowldege, 'I hope they have plenty of aspirin.'

'You don't have to worry about headaches when your skull's 25 centimetres thick!' said Captain Fact.

'Very interesting,' said Knowledge,
'but they're not helping us find Tricky's mother.'

'That's just where you're wrong, Knowledge,' said
Captain Fact. 'Ker-Fact! Pachycephalosaurs are
herbivores just like Triceratops, so we're looking in
the right sort of place.'

'I just love herbivores,' said Knowledge. 'They
carry you around, make silly noises and, best of all,
they don't want to eat you.'

Just then Captain Fact noticed that the Pachycephalosaurs had stopped in their tracks and were nervously sniffing the air. Tricky was squeaking again.

'There's only one problem with herbivores, Knowledge,' said Captain Fact. 'They attract carnivores.'

'Yes,' said Knowledge, 'like that one over there. Look, it's got funny little arms.'

'And great big teeth – it's a Tyrannosaurus Rex!' shouted Captain Fact. As they fled his forehead began to throb . . .

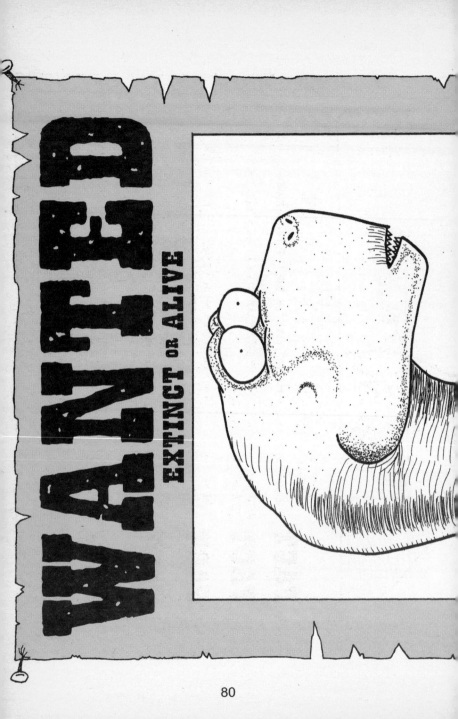

TYRANNOSAURUS REX

FACT TYRANNOSAURUS REX MEANS 'KING OF THE TYRANT LIZARDS'.

FACT A T REX'S STRIDE IS FIVE METRES LONG – FURTHER THAN MOST PEOPLE CAN LONG JUMP!

FACT T REX'S HANDS HAD TWO FINGERS WHICH WEREN'T MUCH BIGGER THAN YOURS!

FACT ONE OF THE MOST FAMOUS T REX FOSSILS IS SIX METRES HIGH. THE CREATURE WOULD HAVE WEIGHED UP TO SEVEN TONNES. IT'S IN THE FIELD MUSEUM IN CHICAGO AND IS NICKNAMED 'SUE'.

FACT T REX PROBABLY COULDN'T RUN VERY FAST AND SO WOULD HAVE EATEN DEAD ANIMALS IF IT HAD THE CHANCE.

FACT BUT T REX WASN'T THE BIGGEST PREDATORY DINOSAUR EVER: THAT WAS GIGANTOSAURUS, WHOSE SKULL WAS AS BIG AS A MAN.

Captain Fact and Knowledge found themselves backed into a corner. Things were looking bleak.

'This is just like Dinosaur Attack III,' whispered Captain Fact. 'What happens now?'

'G-g-game over,' stuttered Knowledge.

CHAPTER 9
SNAP HAPPY

SUDDENLY THE EARTH began to rumble and a huge cloud of dust could be seen in the distance. It was heading straight for them!

'What now?' asked Knowledge. 'Don't tell me his brothers and sisters have been invited to the superhero buffet as well.'

The Tyrannosaurus Rex stopped in its tracks.

'It's a herd of Triceratops! We're saved!' shouted Captain Fact, as his toes began to curl . . .

The Tyrannosaurus Rex roared defiantly then pounded off as fast as its legs could carry it.

'Coward!' shouted Knowledge. 'Typical playground bully, when the going gets tough . . .'

'Not so fast, Knowledge,' warned Captain Fact. 'One of the Triceratops is charging straight for us!'

'Well, it's been great knowing you, Captain Fact. Tricky, so sorry we couldn't help you find your mother,' said Knowledge.

'Not even the Power of Fact can get us out of this one,' said Captain Fact grimly.

Captain Fact and Knowledge braced themselves for the inevitable collision. But at the last second the Triceratops screeched to a halt.

'Mamma!' said Tricky.

'It's Tricky's mother,' said
Knowledge, 'I can't believe
we've found her!'
    'Isn't it sweet?' said Captain
Fact as he prepared the Fact
Watch Camera.

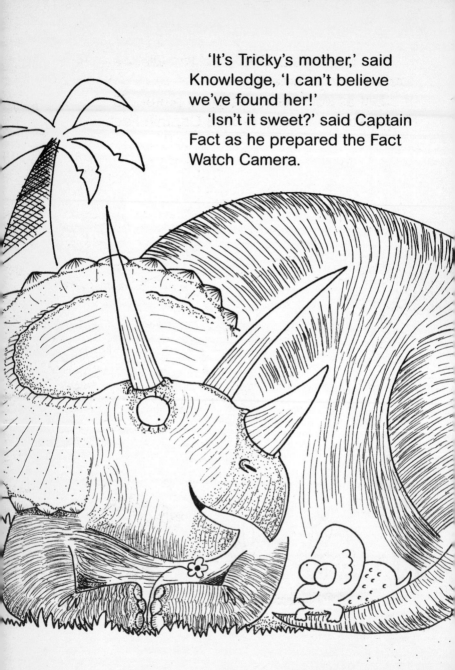

'Yes, but I'm starving,' said Knowledge, 'when are we going home?'

'Just as soon as we've got a picture for Professor Miniscule,' replied Captain Fact.

After Captain Fact had taken his photo, Tricky invited them to hop on the back of her mum.

'I think she's offering us a lift back to the time machine,' said Captain Fact as he jumped aboard.

And so they set out across the pre-historic landscape for the final time.

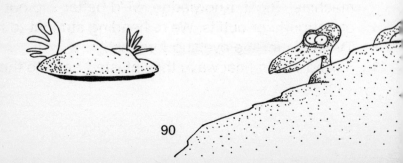

CHAPTER 10
AND NOW THE WEATHER

IN NO TIME at all they were in sight of the Past Blaster 3000.

Captain Fact shook Tricky's paw. 'I'm going to miss you, Tricky, but it's best that you're here where you belong with your mother.'

'My last dog biscuit,' said Knowledge handing over a slightly chewed, curry-flavoured doggy treat, 'in case you get peckish.' Then he gave Tricky a huge hug.

'I never thought I'd see you hugging a dinosaur,' said Captain Fact as they stepped aboard the time machine. 'Right, Knowledge, we'd better slip out of our superhero outfits. We're heading straight to the TV studio for the evening forecast.'

And with a final wave they blasted back to the 21st century.

After a last bout of shuddering and shaking the Past Blaster 3000 ground to a halt.

'Welcome back to the 21st century – *fizz*,' crackled Professor Miniscule over the intercom. 'I've got some good news and some bad news. The good news is you're in the right time zone – *crackle* – the bad news is . . .'

'We're in the Boss's office!' screamed Captain Fact. 'Professor Miniscule, get rid of the time machine at once! Knowledge, let's get out of here!'

As the Past Blaster 3000 vanished, the Boss rubbed his eyes in stunned disbelief.
'I must be losing it. I could have sworn I just saw Thornhill and Puddles climbing out of a time machine,' thought the Boss. 'It can't have been. I'm over-tired, I need the day off.'

As the Boss booked himself another holiday Cliff and Puddles ran into the Make-up Department.

'Cliff and Puddles! Where have you been?' asked Lucy. 'I've been looking everywhere for you. Do you remember that baby dinosaur?'

'Er . . . yes,' said Cliff.

'Well, Captain Fact and Knowledge managed to take her back to her mother!' said Lucy, holding up the evening paper. 'I think Captain Fact looks particularly dishy in this picture. I'd love to go out on a date with him!'

Cliff blushed bright red as he and Puddles stepped through the door to the TV studio.

And so, with Tricky safely back with her mother in the Cretaceous period, Cliff Thornhill and Puddles were back doing what they did worst – the weather.

TOMORROW MORNING THERE WILL BE A RUMBLE OF THUNDER. NOT AS LOUD AS A HERD OF TRICERATOPS, THOUGH . . . WHOOPS!

Until the next crisis . . .

COMING SOON!

CAPTAIN FACT's

CREEPY-CRAWLY ADVENTURE
AND
EGYPTIAN ADVENTURE